T0160930

IN COUNTRY

For my mother,
Katherine Knurek Martin
(May 21, 1952–December 22, 2014)

Contents

III

In Country

Sad mothers gaze at the flagpole which is wetted
by the sun. Stars forever. Stars at night.
—Fadhil al-Azzawi

we called it. Called it
  like my uncle called his months

in Saigon. Slow addition
     of nights & days away

from the States. *Three-sixty-five*

  and a wakeup, we'd say. *The sand-*
box. The desert. Over

there. Or just
there. Where, missing my own mother,
     I pushed an Iraqi boy from a courtyard

    while his mother watched.
    Where I wore, sewn to the right

     shoulder-sleeve, the flag—real

red, white, & blue, star field

    facing forward—
like guidon bearers
     hoisting the colors

 in my country's
  Revolution. *When worn*
    in this manner, Army Regs say, *it gives the effect*

    of the flag flying in the breeze
     as the wearer moves forward.

In country,
  Mongols turned the Tigris red,
  then black with ink. *Uruk*,

Sumerian city which *Iraq*,
              some say, comes from. From

          the Latin, *contra*—opposite,
                          against. In country

      Mashoof canoes
      drifted through marshes

              of green reeds—original
                              Eden. In country

                      marbled teal
          & black-crowned
          night heron. In country
  a Black Hawk hovered

          above the rebuilt ziggurat
of Ur
  for photographs. Just clicks

  from base, some boys burned

a flag on a street:
              dozens of feet

  stomping & jumping
upon the fiery cloth

  like a broken trampoline. Toby Keith
played for us

in country. We ate,
      with Iraqi soldiers,

Thanksgiving dinner
   in country. Countdowns
         we kept in ink

      on cardboard walls of naked women
ripped from shiny

   magazines. *Country
   matters,* Hamlet called it.

In country,
   Iraqis took holidays

         near the always-blue
   Dokan Lake. *All fucking day,*

            a soldier said, when asked,
            How long you been

      in country? A man

      in a Baqubah café
   crossed his legs, lifted

his sandal's heel for me to see
   as he held his tea
in country.
   Two shoes thrown

at my commander-in-chief

in country. The farmer said
            he thinks
                  America

      when planes dot
   the sky of his country. In country,
      kids ran off

after throwing rocks
    which pelted our armored trucks.
  Our gunners,
      in country, ducked

      & yelled
at the kids' footsteps

          down alleys where curtains

      rustled from open windows. Yelled
          as a woman walked out with a broom,

              looked at our trucks,
          then beat dust

      from a long rug sprawled
over a plastic chair—which,

      as she hit it, shook
              & shook.

I

stars gather again to watch the war
—W.S. Merwin

Burn Detail

The generator's hum drowns
    the small splash

      as I pour JP8
from the jug's mouth. Toilet-

paper sods, the softening
    shit—all of it

      rises in each rusted drum.
The new rumor: home

for Christmas. Stack holds his breath,
    drops a cardboard square

      with a tail of yellow flame—fire
crawls to the steel's edge.

The other rumor: patrols
    for January's election.

      On the ordnance bunker
we blew in the valley—

rockets by the hundreds, piles
    of green mortars, some stuck

      like cones in the dirt—
Spoon said the blast was

an orange Goodyear blimp. First,
    we saw the fire burst,

      & then we heard
thunder. In the winding alley

where the sewage-river basks
        all day in the sun:

        a small girl in a red dress
specked with violets saw me

& screamed. She ran
        through the doorway

        of a gray lace sheet.
The trash-pit burns in silence—

some nights, with buckets of water,
        we douse its white glow

        to give them no place to aim.
Turning from the flames

I stir each drum's fire
        with the shovel we don't use

        to dig. Doc had his first dream
of a boom. He woke us yelling,

Gear up, get out. We promised
        it was nothing. Awake,

        Spoon stood to feed
the baby camel-spider

he'd caught & kept
        in the aquarium

        we'd found in Jalawla's dump.
Only, Spoon said,

an imagined boom, & with tweezers
        he pulled a half-dead fly

       from one of the yellow
stick-paper coils

hanging like a streamer
       from the ceiling of the tent.

Frisking Two Men in Sadiyah

Kenson says to search them
since they've watched us all day

from a doorway. I go down
to the dirt on one knee, begin
where the thin beige dishdasha

grazes the ankle. My palms
then fingers climb as if the leg's

a rope. Kenson points his rifle;
mine's slung across his back.
This man, maybe sixty,

doesn't take his hazel eyes
off my face & as I reach where

my right knuckles brush
the scrotum's loose weight, he doesn't
blink. I frisk the other leg, stand—

forehead level with his gray stubble chin,
his smoky breath. I pat the torso,

pat the outstretched armpits, pat
the breast-pocket's cigarette pack,
then lean into what looks like a hug,

slide hands down his back,
my vest's six magazines press

his stomach. He sees through
the black ballistic glasses I wear—
all of us wear—for explosions,

for sunlight, & as I squeeze
both arms through his sleeves,

I think he'll be the one,
after hundreds, to spit gently
on my cheek. I tilt my head.

A few feet behind: Kenson—
just to see he's there. When I step away,

the man studies my face as if
to put it all to memory. All
I want: to grab my rifle from Kenson,

but the other man steps forward,
lifts his arms, & waits for my hands to begin.

Indirect Fire

—FOB Cobra

1.

   Wolfey's head inside
his duffel.   He's looking
for headphones. *It's hell,*

   I'd said, *hearing*

that Pantera-sounding-shit
   blast from your laptop speakers. His head's

in that duffel still when
   we hear the air

outside swallow
itself.   & the explosion, the
boom: my stomach

pumped quick
   with one quick

wind-gust.

2.

   Get down, he whispers as if
it matters.
   We get down

like dogs because the sandbags

we'd stacked outside,
   half-assed,

are five-feet high.   & then

we hug the floor.

3.

   From here, I see
a mound of baby powder left

where Lemon likes to stand

& shake too much
   on his crotch.

4.

With our rifles we run
from the tent, heads down,

   my hand on Wolfey's back

   in the desert night so dark

I can't see his lunging shape.

   Gathered against

Hesco walls of dirt,
our platoon crouches,

silent, listening for the next noise metal

      in the sky will make.

5.

   I turn the switch—the Nods
click.   Now I see:

my platoon's collage
      of camouflaged bodies:

static-green,
   wedged against
dirt-barriers.

It is just
      our first. We wait.

Everyone
shuts up. Everyone

   holds still.

Some men hold on to the gravel.

Fort Knox

to wait
to form a line to form a line to form a line . . .
—Randall Jarrell

This is the line
for showers where men

hold soap cases over
their dicks. This is the line

for the rappel tower
where men look at the sky

then fall. This is the line
for phones where men

have two minutes to call
home. This is the back

of each head: the hairline
squared or rounded. The nicks

& moles on necks. On marches,
the shift of shoulders. This

is the line for the pit where men
hold sandbags above

their heads. This is the line
for shots & vaccinations

where a man, so tired,
walked off with a syringe

hanging from his arm
like a string.

Operation New Dawn

—12/15/2011, Tempe, AZ

          Before Iraq I had a problem speaking
          my name to women I liked in loud bars
          or silent grocery cereal aisles

          because *Hugh* sounds like
          the second-person singular *You*
          so I spent much time
          placing emphasis on that first

consonant that's soft as breath,
but still they'd say *Who?* or *What?* or
Q? Before Iraq I watched the Shock

& Awe in a college campus housing
living room where friends spoke
that first consonant with
assurance & force as they asked

          what kind of tank that was
          or what kind of bomb just
          exploded in that dark Baghdad

          skyline, they'd say my name
          since I was the living room's military
          expert, & I'd say *Bunker-*
          Buster, Bradley Fighting Vehicle,

Tomahawk Missile, although for all of it
I had no idea like I had no idea
I'd be there within the year.

Meanwhile we drank beers
& said *Shock and Awe*
for the rush those quick syllables
made falling from our mouths. After

Iraq, I read how an Iraqi man
said, *To tell you the truth,*
I was neither shocked nor awed.

In Iraq in Sadiyah where yellow
flowers climbed a mud wall
& date palm fronds stretched
sharp in the sky, an Iraqi man yelled,

Hey, Mister—they called us *Mister*
or *Soldier*—& shook my hand
then said *Saddam, Saddam,*

& spat on the road. Saddam's eldest,
he told me, Uday, took a girl—
the man's sister, maybe
his friend's sister, maybe

        his neighbor's sister—took her
        for a weekend, dropped her
        back in town but of course

        there's more, of course he stood
        half an hour: telling with both hands,
        his broken English, both of us sweating
        in July where those date palms, those

flowers the color of sunlight
made no shade. The story ended
when he said, covered in sweat

from the telling, she'd doused herself
in gasoline & to show what he meant:
he threw his open hands up
& down his body's length like

        someone frantically fanning off
        heat. *Mister, thank you*, he whispered.
        Your name, your name, but it was there

on my ballistic vest Velcroed
in black: *Martin,* he said, *Martin,* he said
& said as he left. That was also
the week when, early one morning,

a platoon of us stood in a family's
courtyard under stars after
we'd searched for wires, detonators,

bags of cell phones, & Captain said
to look on that roof where
folded blankets & bags of what
were piled with rakes & shovels.

Lt. told, I'll call him *Champ*—
a state wrestling champ—to look,
& Champ jumped, grabbed the stiff

mud-roof's edge. As he swung
one leg to catch the boot's heel
to wall he fell, arms flailing,
& plates—handmade plates—

stacked on an end table shattered
against the concrete floor. We,
the Misters, standing in all corners

of that yard where the family slept,
scoffed, some of us, myself
included, turned away as if to ignore
our little disaster, but

at the same time, the older woman—
the mother—sobbed, loud, louder
than when we'd zip-cuffed

her son minutes ago. Captain,
always carrying wads of cash,
pushed a handful of dinars
to the woman's face & she slapped

it away, turned her back.
With the terp speaking, he followed
& insisted she take it. Back,

that night, at the FOB I sat
in the Morale, Welfare,
& Recreation room, which was just
the large living room

        of a dead Iraqi Colonel's home,
        & scrolled, as I often did, the names
        of the dead on CNN: its *Home and Away*

        Casualty List where a white dot
        on America's map meant
        dead soldier: name, rank, place
        of birth, & as I'd zoom out,

the dots would blur together
like human lights from space
at night or a map to show

where the country suffered
a heavy downfall of snow.
After Iraq, I wondered how
anyone ever slept after we left

        their homes, if they ever slept
        the same at all. Also: there was a van
        our 113 hit, head on—we, driving

        forty in black-out, Night-Vision;
        the van going fifty—& when
        our convoy stopped, we looked inside:
        thirteen, we counted, dead. The driver's face

flat to the steering wheel as if
he'd been trying, I'd thought,
to dive through it. Day two, too,

another, a truck—Wiley asking, *Martin,*
you shoot? You shoot? He meant shoot
that truck that'd sped toward our FOB
with sparks spraying from its tailgate

      like small fireworks as our platoon
      leaned, rifles aimed, on the mud berm
      & fired at what was just

      some man & his son dragging
      steel rebar from the truck's
      bed to their home. We'd shot
      until the truck stopped. After Iraq

in a Houston club where velvet light
washed the room under dim blue
spotlights, a black-haired woman

I'd met on my lap, so close
I smelled coconut lotion, asked my name
& she heard me say, *Who* or *You.*
You, she said, *you—your name,*

      but with the bass & boom I yelled
      what I'd been yelling for years,
      Like Hugh Hefner, & then she laughed

      a perfect smile glowing white
      which began a talk of her life
      living at the mansion with Hefner—
      It was only six months, she said.

I told her I'd traded a *Playboy*
for a Kurdish soldier's Iraqi Army hat.
She smiled. *Should we be there?* After

Iraq I sat in an American
desert cold from too much air-
conditioning & watched the End
of Mission Ceremony—named

Operation New Dawn: two soldiers
took down, then rolled up,
the United-States-Forces-Iraq flag:

one held it horizontal while the other
pulled on the camouflage casing,
what we called the *flag condom*,
then they marched off, off-camera,

as the Army Band played a patient,
low brass. My parents named me
after my father's father who died

when I was seven so I never
had the chance to ask if he'd had
this problem, but I know my mother
had no problem yelling *Hugh Joseph*

Martin, which meant I'd done something
bad. I drank with the boys from my platoon,
after Iraq, & more than a few times

I'd drink with Champ—in fact,
one January, a few of us sat
in the hot tub he'd bought
for the deck he'd built

at his house just outside Canton,
where we shoveled deep snow off
the whirlpool's cover & huddled

down in that water up to our necks:
some of us from Akron, Green,
Reminderville, & that night it was—
I'll call him *Mister*, though by then

we only used first-names—Mister who
brought up those broken plates,
which we'd all forgotten,

   & that woman: *she wouldn't even take*
   our money, he said & we all laughed
   at Champ, who laughed, too.
   She wouldn't even take our money! You

fucking stooge, he said, then stood up,
flung out his arms & fell just
as Champ had, fell like the snow

on the screen & the flakes
on the water's small foam waves.
You klutz, he said. But that,
that was a different story.

Wave of Bombings

16 More Killed in Wave of Bombings in Iraq
—*New York Times*, 7/17/13

There was never a black bowling ball, a burning fuse
waving its tail. No bombs but

in things. No IEDs but
in things: the mound
of beige bricks; the soft sand-waves

beside the road; the bridge above
the muddy Diyala. There was never

water, never:
splash. For our crew

of four, there was—not
a wave—the punch of wind, a film
of dust, shrapnel in

Kenson, the Humvee. On patrols we'd wave
to the children. Some would wave;

some would run. We would run,
after bombs, in waves
as if to prove we still

had legs. Don't think of the thousands of legs
stretched together at ball games
to see & be

the wave. It will happen as someone is eating
or opening a window or walking

dully along. In my case, driving the M114 up-armored Humvee
dully along. Always a ball

of flame but not the ocean-
flop to shore, nor

the tsunami's rising
ridge of sea. When we,
the alive ones, returned

to fluorescent light, soft
applause, they stood around us
like a parted sea

& they waved small flags
on short wooden sticks.

Iraq Good

The small boy smiles, kicks roundhouses
across the potholed road, says, *Van Damme*

good? & I say, *Yes, Van Damme good.*
   The boy punches the warm air while we,

   on the street for hours, outside
the Sadiyah police compound walled

with Hescos higher than our gunners'
   heads, pace circles around the trucks.

   Two other boys, maybe nine or ten,
chop each other, gently,

with knife-hands, & one turns, says,
   No good Saddam, Saddam

   very no, & he points to his sandal's heel,
Saddam no. & so

it went: *Bruce Lee good, Zamzam good,*
   falafel good, even

   Michael Jackson good, even *Bush good*, even *America*
very good. We stood,

speaking on ground where written words
   were first made, where Enheduanna

   wrote her poems, blunt reed
on wet clay, the clay that made the walls

those children slept behind at night,
   that filled the Hescos behind our backs.

We leaned, a few feet from the boys,
against Humvees—two-hundred grand

each—made in Indiana. Insurgents
were paid—we knew—to blow one apart:

five-hundred U.S. cash. Sometimes,
as the boys spoke to each other,

their Arabic muffled
by passing traffic & muezzin calls,

we'd talk among ourselves, asking,
just steps from the boys, which one might,

in five or ten years or less,
fight us. Still, these silences, brief,

would break when one of the boys
might point to our rifles, muzzles

aimed at the road, the red-dot scopes
clipped to the carrying handles,

& say, *Laser . . . good*, then point
to our dark sunglasses, say, *X-ray yes, good*,

&, although we'd agree,
there was really no *laser*, no *X-ray*,

but if we kept those boys there,
talking, on that street as evening came,

we'd be, for the moment, okay
if only we kept it going: *Ali Baba*

*no good, chicken good, Sadiyah good, Iraq
good, & good, & good.*

All of This Ammo

—*Camp Udairi, Kuwait*

is ours. Inside the tent
Strom pops open a can
of .50 & unfolds

the long chain with both hands,
lifting it from the box,
trying to curl its weight,

holding it over his head
& setting it like a bronze stole
around his neck. His *scarf,*

he says before someone takes
a picture. Soon, all of us begin
lifting this chain

onto our shoulders,
posing for pictures,
hardly able to stand straight

or take it off. All of us
had only shot,
by the thousands,

plastic men in America
on forts named for famous
generals; men whose red rifles

were painted over their plastic
chests. Before the photo,
we straighten our backs,

our slouching necks,
loosen the strain
on our faces & act as if

the chain is just as heavy
as silk. But after the flash,
we lean over, curse the weight,

the tips of the rounds
on our skin, & beg each other
to help, to take the damn thing off.

Sunday in the City of Oranges

—Baqubah, Iraq

1.

Kenson yells, *Tell him back up.*
　This farmer—he might
　　　　　　be ninety—wears a black & white
　　　　checkered keffiyeh loose on his head.
In one hand he holds a long shovel,
　　　　rusted spade up, & he stumbles toward us & shouts.

The three voices in the groves:
　　　　　　our best terp, Basheer,
　　　　　　　translates as the man yells
　　　　　& Kenson yells to Basheer
　　　　　　　& Basheer yells back
　　　　　　　　to the man & on & on.

2.

He's just a farmer. He say Americans blow up his tractor.
　　　Tell him to fucking back up.
He say there is nothing here, nothing in these groves.
　　　Tell him back off, that's a warning, tell him, Basheer.
He say he wants payment for his tractor.
　　　Tell him keep his hands out, stay the fuck back.
He say this is his farm. He is no Ali Baba.

3.

　Last week, huddled
around one slow desktop computer,

　we saw: the girl held a leash,
a nude man on the ground.

Spoon blurted out, *Those idiots—*

we're more fucked now.

Basheer scoffed, *I will tell you*
about torture.

4.

The old man could not care less
    about the ten rifles
pointed his way. He turns,

holds his shovel like a staff & hobbles off
    between the date palms

    as Basheer translates his loud muttering.

5.

    He say you Americans and your planes ruin my sky.
He say—this man is crazy—he can't see his sky.
    He say silly American dogs—he say we, Iraqis, invented farming.
He say go away. Do not touch any of my trees.

6.

Before the man walks off,
    Spoon runs over & frisks him.

    The man mumbles, *Silly American dog silly American dog*
until Spoon's done.

When he's gone, we keep walking.
We listen to our boots in the tall grass.
    We listen to bird-calls. We find nothing.

As the date palms end,
>   we arrive at a field, tall yellow grass,
>   & see, from across it,

a different copse
  of groves: oranges, hundreds,
>   nested against green leaves
>   & they look like little
>   orbs of flame.
>   We stop here.

Basheer says, *They call Baqubah*
>   *City of Oranges.*
>   He chews his soggy cigar.

7.

  Our third day in country:
we'd thought
>   he was only waving, *hello,*
>   some local custom—his whole

>   right hand open, inches
>   from my face—then I saw:

>   the pinky gone
>   below the knuckle.
That's how I met Basheer.
>   He said, *Welcome to Iraq.*

Suspicious Duffel Bag, LSA Anaconda

That bag's not mine, someone says. We watch it
as if it might move. The bag's a green
island in the motor-pool gravel. The bag's
left over from some tired battalion
that boarded a plane to Kuwait. The bag's
full of some private's unused cold-weather
camo. The bag's like the one, dropped
in the dining hall by a local worker, that blew
in Mosul. Men step from their tents to see
the bag. *Oh, come on*, Kenson says. *It's just some
guy's shit*. But no one will walk to the bag,

pull open its flaps, see what's inside. *You know
whose bag?* Some sergeant says to two men walking
from chow. They stop & walk the long way
around our tents. *No*, one guy says. *But that bag
looks suspicious*. In the silence, I can hear the bag's
brief explosion. Its spray of steel shards, nails.
The green nylon shred to scraps. The bag's
stuffed with little Purple Hearts. The bag's
stuffed with titanium prosthetic legs
etched with American flags. The bag's filled
with Servicemember Life Insurance forms.

The bag's full of little men dressed
in Class As who pace down sidewalks
& knock on doors. The bag's full of Names
of the Dead newspaper clippings. Lt. says,
I'm not taking a chance. He calls base headquarters
about the bag. *I promise you*, Kenson says,
it's just some dumb fuck's bag of porn.
Lt. asks, *You want to check?* No one,
not even Kenson, will approach the bag.
The bag is like that one, full of tomatoes,
we blew in Balad. The bag's like the shoebox

that blew & knocked out Smith. Four men
from EOD order us to back away from the bag.
The bag was stolen from the PX. The bag
was dropped by a local worker. The bag
was gently filled with a large mortar round wired
to blow by the same worker, watching,
on this base that's built like a city. We sit
against the bunker's concrete wall. *Fire
in the hole*, a sergeant yells. *All this*, Kenson says,
cuz some dumbass left his bag. Bag of gear. Bag
of porn. Bag of legs. Gone. One sound.

Sorrow Awareness Training

—Fort Bragg, NC

Our company sits on the gymnasium bleachers & we sip watery coffee from Styrofoam cups. We've had briefings on how to drive in the desert; how to stop a sucking chest wound; how to conduct yourself near a mosque; how to fill out an SGLV 8286 for Servicemembers' Group Life Insurance. But Captain says that the Department of Defense has ordered all soldiers to attend Sorrow Awareness Training. "For instance, say your buddy dies to an IED," Captain yells from the gym floor. "Or say you accidentally shoot two civilians during a firefight." & then he splits us into our four-man squads. Each squad has a training NCO; ours is "Old Stan": Sergeant Stanton, who joined the Guard the year I was born. Stanton thinks it's silly, but he says, "Just drive on! Drive on! I've seen stranger shit before . . . Okay, say Kenson here's been shot." Old Stan makes eye contact with each of us. "You've reacted, returned fire, now you're back at base and you find out from Doc he's dead." He stares. Then he reads from the form, "First thing you got to do is cry." Sergeant Mays, our .50-Gunner, laughs, "I ain't going to fucking cry. This is dumb—" Stanton cuts him off. "Wait there, Sergeant, these are DOD orders and if you don't comply, you ain't shipping out. Would you like a No-Go?" Mays smiles & shakes his head. Stanton suggests maybe Kenson should lie down, close his eyes. "It might," Stanton says, "make it easier to visualize." Kenson, tired as any of us, says, "Sure, Sergeant, good idea!" He stretches out on the gym floor, folds his arms over his chest, closes his eyes. "Okay, I'm dead." Stanton looks at the stack of sheets on his clipboard. "Now, guys, here's the scenario: you've been in combat with this man. You know his wife, you know his baby girl, and he's gone—boom. Bullet to the chest." The three of us look at each other. Mays finally speaks, "Okay, give me a few. I'm going to get this." "That's right," Stanton says. "You have to learn to mourn, or how else you going to deal with this?" Mays stands up, says, "Going to use the latrine." He walks off. Groups of men sit all across the bleachers & gym floor. Some talk to the training NCO. Some stare hard at the walls. Some close their eyes. Minutes later Mays jogs toward us across the floor. He grins wide with his right hand stuffed in his cargo pocket. "Sergeant Stanton," he says. "There's no SOP about how we cry, right?" Stanton looks at the sheet, "Not that I know of—just got to cry to get the Go." Mays pulls his hand from the right pant-leg cargo pocket & holds out two onions from the mess hall next door. "Let's fucking cry!" He tosses me an onion & it hits my chest. Stanton calls over the Captain. "Sir, these guys are using onions. Now I don't see any regulations about how the men come to cry, so I said that's okay." The Captain looks at us as we hold the onions. "Well," he says. "I don't know of any regulations but I'm not sure they're taking the training seriously." Stanton opens his mouth to speak but the Captain cuts him off—"What the hell is this soldier doing? Sleeping?" Stanton shakes his head, "Oh, no, no, sir! He's dead. We thought it'd be better to visualize the KIA—might help make the training more real." The Captain walks to the middle of the gym floor. "Listen up," he yells. All the chatter dies out. "A small addendum to the procedure: I want one soldier in each squad to play dead. Sergeant Stan here gave us that good idea." He looks around the gym, nods, "Okay, boys? One man plays dead." Mays lifts a Leatherman from the back of his belt & begins cutting the onion while he holds it to the floor. He reaches out with a half, & after I open my hand, he sets it on my palm. As the Captain walks off, the other soldiers turn to their groups, & all at once, across the floor & bleachers, men lean back, recline—some of them cross one boot over the other. As Kenson snores, his chest rising beneath the desert camouflage uniform, Mays & I wait, holding the halves to our faces.

Man on a Cart

He holds two blue reins
strapped to a mule's bridle.

Nothing—I look, I look—
  in the cart but dust.

  I step into the road & the man
stands in the cart. He shouts.

His red keffiyeh's wet
  to his forehead. He points

  up the road. *La,*
I say. *La. La.*

Someone found something
  in the ground up the road.

  No one can go up the road.
Blue One blocks it

from the other end. Blue Two
  blocks it from the market.

  I have no way
to tell him this. He yells.

He whips the reins. The mule
  kicks. I push my rifle sideways

  to the mule's neck. I say *La*
many times. I say *Fucking go,*

go, away . . .
  The mule's front hooves

clap the pavement. There's a crowd:
maybe twenty men on the corner.

When he shakes the reins, again,
   to pass, with my boot I stomp

   the bald front tire. The cart
rocks back an inch.

The mule dips its neck, takes two
   short steps. Sweat runs along my leg.

   I kick the tire again, look away,
& it's then the man decides

to go. I aim to shoot but don't.
   The mule lurches past.

   The crowd yells. There's laughter.
So I just lunge, lunge

at them all. *Imshi*, I say. *Imshi*.
   I swing the muzzle

   at their stares. Men duck, back away,
& some—not sure

if they should raise their arms or run—
   say, *Mister, no, Mister, no.*

   They know I won't shoot
but they slowly walk

in all directions down
   alleys & roads as I keep

   pointing the rifle until
all of them are gone,

until no one's watching
what I do, or don't.

Lana

Never stare at the women,
      they told us in training. Instead

         I stare at six half-sunk spare tires

in the creek across the road.
      A woman walks,

in my periphery, all black, all
  abaya—it's all,

it seems, I ever see—against
         a landscape all sunlight. Straight

toward our truck—machinegun
  manned by Spoon,
         pointed north to tilled fields, low

    yellow hills, specks
of desert-bush. Basheer, our terp,

steps into the street
      to meet her.

We're parked, a perimeter—*scan*
       your sector, they told us

    in training—our platoon of four gun-trucks,
    around the Jalawla hospital

  where wounded Iraqi soldiers wait

for the medevac
      Black Hawk. When Basheer speaks,

47

I turn, see the woman's face, powdered
        & pale, as she talks, her hands

flailing from the linen toward Basheer,
the trucks, the hospital.

The shawl falls back
  from her forehead
       & she grasps the edges
  with both hands, pulls it

so I only see her mouth, nose, eyes traced
  with black liner.

       I stand between our truck
   & the Iraqi soldiers' white Toyota pickup

  & scan the creek clogged
         with black plastic bags that float,
      I think, like water lilies. *Attention*

to detail, they told us in training,
  & as I watch the bags in the stream

       inch west, the woman stops speaking.
  She walks, so slowly I can hear

pebbles scrape
      beneath her sandals,
  to the pickup's bed,

two meters to my four o'clock, which just means
  a little to my right.

      We hear a tractor's engine
from somewhere in the hills,
      faint traffic from downtown. Still,

while I watch the tires & bags
across the street, I can see

the woman's shape as she stares

at the truck's bed, but I won't turn
or look because I know
the woman's son is there, a son

who hasn't been dead
for more than an hour.

She stands near the truck's cab, her body inches

from the bed, & I know she sees his face
since I'd held
one of his legs—bare heel, back

of the knee—in my hands
& set him headfirst, there were no more

stretchers, on the dusty aluminum.

The woman just stares.
I want to curse the heat,
the shit-stream, the whole sector I've watched,

like other sectors,
& since I want
to slam my face
into the Humvee's hood,

I turn so I can feel my legs, the loose
gravel beneath my boots,

& I see her looking down to where

a green wool army blanket—Doc
had placed it over him—

covers the boy to his shoulders.

When she moves from the truck & back
   to Basheer, she mutters
         quick phrases, then spits,

  & walks off down the road.

Basheer, always in a cheap,
         green Kevlar-vest—it probably

wouldn't stop a pistol round—paces over
   & I glance at his graying mustache,

         the wide sunglasses shading his eyes.

            He says, "Her name is Lana."
            & then he slips his hands—

he always does this—through the open spaces

            beside the vest's collar & just lets them
            hang, his elbows

at his sides like wings. But because

I've spent months with Basheer, because
         he never shuts up, because he chain-smokes

         & tells jokes so bad we laugh, because
            he told us how some British General

had also said, after The Great War,

he'd come to Baghdad as a liberator, I ask, "That

was all?"

                        He glances at the sky,
            looks right at me, "He was oldest
        of family. She tell me"—& he stares south

to fields for miles—"She tell me, *please,*

        please thank America
            for giving my dead boy."

    He sips from his canteen,
                    swings open the Humvee's rear
                    passenger door,
                        steps inside & sits & closes his eyes.

———————————————————

I stare across the road
            & think I hear the chopper's rotors somewhere

    beyond the hills
                    but no green machine
        comes rising out of that horizon.

        Just a warm wind, & beyond that
                        the broad blue glare.

    I hear in my head Basheer
            say her name & I scan the stream,

                    the tires & the plastic bags.
                        The tires & the plastic bags.

II

.50-Cal. Gunner: A Sequence

I. Anthem

1.

All day I aim at date palms.

    The hood's covered
with dried stains: dip, coffee

I've spit. Dalton always yelling from the hole,
    Not on my truck, dick.

Dust, here.
    Dust there.
How many duds don't blow,

I don't know. Inside the Kevlar another song
stuck. Even over

the constant mosque music.

    I'm into having sex.
    Not into making love. (But I'm not

    having. Not making . . .
    Dalton says it's my anthem.)

2.

My wish: to make Devices

        Exploded

    Improvised.

I keep both thumbs on the butterfly.

This camouflage keeps

    my vitals very much part

of the sand I stare down all day. Lt. says,
        The .50 should make people unhappy.

At home, they don't know all I do:

aim at date palms.

3.

Been hit with a few shells.
But I don't walk with a limp. (But mostly

we drive. Mostly,
we drive . . .

        & I aim at date palms.)

I saw what it said
in all that fine print

    below Mission

    Accomplished: accomplished,

of course, but please send

        four thousand (plus)
        body bags.

        Bring them back, please.
        No empties.

II. 0000–0400 Hours: Guard Duty with Elbow

—for BDJ

1.

All shift he yaps, chucks gravel at dogs.

   They weave between
the triple-stacked-
razor-wire. I aim

my red-lens light: a dozen eyes, long
       tongues, ribbed fur

brushing concertina.   His arm's sore

so he flips the 240 steel cover up,
   down, open, shut,
   that click,
      click—he won't

shut up.   His father, he tells me, in Seoul,

as a young private
      sitting too close to the stage,
      was knocked unconscious,

briefly,
      by a spinning stripper's foot.

2.

Like Elbow, I joined the Guard

   for Tuition Assistance & to travel,
mostly.   Elbow—that's where

he had the ringworm—remains

on permanent guard duty

due to the concussion
in June. *I don't remember*

   the boom,
he'd said.   *Everyone just needs*, he insists,

   two-hundred milligrams of
   Be-A-Fucking-Man.

3.

He performs his impression—I've seen it

   all war long—
   of the local Imam's voice

blaring from a minaret: high-pitched,

long—it even scares

   the dogs. He sings

   & sings
to kill the time (it's only quiet

when he leaves to piss).
I fake-laugh

   so I can say, *Enough, enough,*

holding my stomach like it hurts.

III. Sandbag Detail

To avoid the sun we dig at dawn.

I hold the shovel.
Ski holds the bag. *Rambo,*

don't bend your back, he says.

The dirt's more stiff
        when we dig at dawn. When done,

        we'll stack the bags like walls

        around the hooch. Like walls

around the chow hall. Like walls

        around the Morale,
        Welfare,

& Recreation Room.

A pallet's always piled

with more bags.
        They wait for fill. Empties

we use for heads. Ski says,
We'll keep filling

until the whole country's

in a bag. So nothing can ever
   hurt us ever.

IV. Iraqi Civil Defense Corps

1.

Just the muzzle & I: we face

   the rear. In the dark I hear

minaret music, yet,
half the time
   it's just from my head. Always wind,

the truck's engine, the yellow
   hills in the light, the stars

   at night (up here,
you can see them

whenever you like). *Kiss the babies,*

Kenson said. *Kill the bad guys.*
     Give the children Charms.

2.

The ICDC
   checkpoint: Iraqi men,

Kalashnikovs, khaki
pants, camo tops.

    ACDC-motherfuckers,
we used to yell like hell.   Now,

they just wave rifles & smokes.

Passing Sadiyah,

kids call me *Rambo*,
Jackie Chan (they cheer when I do

a double-bicep pose).

3.

    Last month, I took Ambien—big
mistake—when Kenson,

on a down-day,
    ripped us from our bunks to load body-bags.

By lunch: six ICDC

in all. Shot
in their sleep. Beds lined behind

Checkpoint Seven

    since the hut's too hot (*hotter*

days, Kenson said, *just think, think*
snow). So now

    all that *ACDC!*—
we just don't.   & the sand's still

    a bitch when it blows.

V. Route Willow, Jalawla Bridge

fake you, ameriki

vietnam street

well make it your graves here

VI. ICDC HQ Building

Up here it's dark but dawn's

   sunlight already hurts. All

our guys are asleep. Except
   Fork: on the eastern ledge,

   he brushes his teeth, spits

   to the courtyard below where,

yesterday,
the fat Iraqi colonel
      sawed, for dinner, the head off

a lamb—*You're not*

to eat that, Captain said.

   As we waited for the thing
to stop twitching,

   the colonel lifted
one hind leg

   so it'd bleed out faster—I thought

   it'd rip right off.

Morning, beautiful,
   Fork says, white toothpaste

streaking down his chin (it's my turn to replace him).

     An Iraqi soldier pacing

the roof's perimeter nods at Fork,

then me.   We know him—Marwan—
always smiling, chain-

smoking, whispering,
Hello, Mister,

   too many times. He's from

Sulaymaniyah—*It sort of looks,*

      Captain said, *like Colorado.*   Locked,

loaded: a Kalashnikov's

   slung across Marwan's back,

its muzzle aimed to the roof.
   Seeing his sleepy eyes, I think
I trust him.

   Fork falls back,

his head on a half-empty ruck,

   pulls the ballistic vest
across his chest like a blanket.

   I slip into my boots,
walk to the ledge,

stepping over & between men, rifles.

   Some sleep, curled,
heads on bundled camo tops. Others

   lay flat, wearing socks
as eye masks.

They have, maybe,

an hour until
   the morning's prayer calls.

VII. Tigris Crossing

          —Balad, Iraq

1.

On Saddam:
    she wishes he'd come back to life

so she could kill him twice.
We hear her story twice.

    She talks to Nina (Nina's not
her real name)

because she won't talk to us.
  Nina's in jeans,

a blue collared blouse—she's our only

female terp.
The Tigris: muddied brown,

bright in the sun.

On living
  last March in Baghdad:

      When she hear fighters coming in sky, Nina says.
       Her family hold their breathing. Their hearts are jumping out.
      The bombs shake them. Three nights they don't sleep.

2.

We wait at this buoyed bridge.

   There might be a bomb: miles
down the road EOD

destroys some suspicious thing—a bag,
   plastic—placed

   at the roundabout's west entrance.

   Our trucks: filled with lumber,

steel bunkbeds, bottled water cases.
   We wait. Up here,

it's hotter
   on the gun. *Just go,*

I want to scream—*fuck it, just go*—

because, after all,
   the bomb's probably fake.

3.

   The woman's in a flowing black abaya.
On her fingers I see

      faint green tribal tats: lines, dots. Skin's
   like my leather
pistol holster but it's her skin.

She doesn't move
   from the mud wall's doorway.

Nina tells all this to Lt. but up

on the gun
I hear the quick
Arabic, then Nina.

> She want America to have night like her family.
> She say she hate those machine in the sky.
> No special effect in America movies are like them.
> Her son say, 'Mama, I don't want night to come.
> I hate the night. I wish we can skip it.'

III

Mini-Mohammad

—Jalawla, Iraq

From this dirt hill, high over town, past the blue
    four-story police compound, the concrete-block

parking lot, the brick city council center
    where the Captain sits as we—four gun-trucks,

platoon of fifteen—wait, patrol on foot, smoke
    at our trucks, sweat in our socks & ballistic vests,

we see him, down among mid-morning
    market crowds shoulder to shoulder before

the noon burns: blur of loose black Adidas pants,
    t-shirt faded with Mickey Mouse's face—

he won't say where (we've asked) he got it—
    & he weaves, waist-high, between women,

the wind from him brushing their abayas,
    the men's dishdashas, passes

sputtering traffic, skips between bumpers,
    slaps his little hand on car-hoods, some tied down

with rope. Some men yell, punch their horns,
    but Mini-Mohammad spins & laughs,

bursts past the turquoise-tiled minaret,
    one lone cow nosing through trash, the vendor shack

where whole roasted chickens glow behind glass,
    the stacked ice pillars pushed on a cart

by the boy who yells, all morning—*Ice, ice!*—
    the dim streams flowing from shops

& homes, inching down each street's edge—
    Mini-Mohammad jumps these, full-speed,

mid-air, legs spread, sandal to hard sand he lands.
    At our truck, Doc says, the Grizzly a bump

in his lip, *I'm about to shoot up an IV bag.* For us, today:
    all day council-detail. Kenson flicks off the sun.

I sip piss-warm water from a half-gallon jug.
    We talk to kids. Kick balls. Take turns sitting

inside the Humvee's shade. Named, week one,
    by Doc—Mini, hardly five-feet tall, Mohammad

is our wish-deliverer, our ten-year-old city salesman,
    spokesman for the plastic-bag-Pepsi-special—

he runs so fast, the cans come cold.
    Against distant minaret music, the hum

of rusted mufflers, we hear *Mister,* then his feet—
    slap-slap—on pavement. *Mister!* He smiles—

those two top teeth chipped from a fall—*Mister,*
    what you like? He stands before Doc,

stares up, *How are you? You want falafel?*
    Chicken? Ice Pepsi? Two—one dollar.

Doc says, *Don't you go to school,*
    little man? Mini-Mohammad waves his hand,

No, Mister, no. You want DVD-
    freaky-freaky? Ice cream? Watch?

From a pant-leg pocket he pulls a beige case,
    opens the suede lid: a silver Rolex. *Mister,*

you sell in Ameriki, I know you sell,
     lots of money . . . Iraq cheap, I give good deal,

for you, five-dollar, you my friend.
     Doc says, *Already got a couple. Get me a bird*

back home, Mini-Mohammad, how about that?
     Doc waves his arms, rifle in one hand,

Bird, airplane. Plane. Up—up there.
     He points at the sky. Mini-Mohammad looks up,

flings out his arms, spins, shades his eyes
     with one hand, scans, & Doc pulls two dollars

from a cargo-pocket. Before we blink, Mini-Mohammad's
     grabbed it, gone—we hear the slap

on the street, his shoulders pumping, the crumpled
     bills in his left hand blowing, then he dissolves

into the market crowds, sometimes crawling, swift,
     between a man's legs, grasping a woman's sleeve,

pulling forward—he's never walked a day in his life.
     We wait for anything. We drench the grips, our rifles'

handguards. We wipe our hands against our long sleeves
     the color of dark mud, sand, crinkled khaki.

Minutes later, to my two-o'clock, past the mechanic shops:
     he runs, lapping the flung-open steel shop-shutters,

the tin shack rooftops, the many boys & men
     sitting on crates, their hands glistening with black grease.

Headlights, bumpers, wires, exhaust pipes, rubber hoses
     hang from the ceilings & walls. Mini-Mohammad's

right arm's raised straight ahead as he gallops, closer,
　　　smiling: a potato bag gripped in his hand, the black

plastic bag—two Pepsis—in the other, his silhouette's
　　　a glare against the brick pile where an IED—we've had fifty

in this town—blew in late June, & as he's closer,
　　　he opens the bag, slips one hand inside & lifts two gray-blue

pulsing heads—pigeons—held tight between his forefinger
　　　& thumb. *Mister! Two for five—you my friend. Two for five!*

Doc yells, *Mohammad brought me some fucking birds—*
　　　& it's east, near the IP checkpoint: I hear it

as Mini-Mohammad squeezes the bag with both hands,
　　　leaves enough space so the birds can stretch their necks,

feathers like smooth ash, open their black beaks hardly
　　　making a murmur. *You like bird,* he says. *Yes?*

Two for five—for you—& what he says next
　　　is muffled by a soft boom. Spoon traverses the .50.

I fling open the armored door, start the engine,
　　　set my rifle beside the gear shift, & Doc jumps in,

slams the door shut as I'm already pushing the pedal.
　　　See you, little man, Doc yells from the open window.

Mini-Mohammad shouts, *Bomb, Mister, bomb?* He stands,
　　　holds, in one hand, the bag of Pepsis, tightens his other

around the birds' necks as they, like Mini-Mohammad, look out
　　　to the gray-black smoke streaked, east, high above the village.

Test Fire

—south of Jalawla

After we drive through
the barren hills
where the earth unrolls

itself for miles, where the soil's
as stale as boxed cookies
sent from the Youngstown

USO, the gunners fire
machineguns at the ridge
wall's face—small

dust-explosions lift
to the sky like faded desert
larks while the rest of us

shoot from our knees, our
chests, as copper casings
rain like loose change

across the dirt, then
as we convoy back
to Cobra from nowhere

the Bedouin come
to collect the shells
& stuff them in sacks

& after they go: only
boot & footprints,
a careful cursive of tire-tracks.

Civilian Notes

—for VLB 1/30/2005

on TV the woman's forefinger stained violet with election ink;

a civilian, I watch from this beige suede sofa;

midnight in Ohio & there's wind & deep snow-sheets outside;

the camera pans past Iraqis standing in lines;

I've studied that date palm through a scope;

I've put my hand on that concrete barrier;

the one-handed man yelled, *it was better with Saddam*;

my right leg's sore from the stiff Humvee pedal;

on your front door I touched the cold window;

I touched the fake-pine wreath with red berries & small poinsettias;

I still hear the muezzin's call;

an Iraqi tailor said, *we are ready for war like you are ready for winter*;

I pissed on the tarmac before we flew home;

the first rocket I ate gravel;

he said, *I want to kill all Americans*;

I drove full speed through roundabouts;

I closed my eyes through bomb-dust;

the women always *wrapped in black, black cloaks, black abayas, black burqas, black veils;*

the handcuffed man spit at my boots;

a reporter says, *some call this The Purple Finger of Freedom;*

your eyes are closed so I turn the volume low;

I don't tell you we called it *The Trigger Finger;*

I searched a van & found squashed lemons beneath a seat;

I searched homes & found foam mattresses stitched with bright flowers;

we blew up bags of onions;

we blew up concrete slabs;

we blew up ordnance from the Iran-Iraq War;

I parked the Humvee beneath apricot trees;

a boy with a toy pistol said, *we play Israelis and Palestinians;*

adjacent to the TV is a mirror on the wall;

the mirror shows the woman with the purple finger;

black & white photos you took in San Juan;

miniature fake-pine with tinsel fluttering from the heat vent;

beside me, you're asleep beneath a fleece blanket;

Spoon could hold the .50 & sleep;

I dumped warm water on my face to stay awake;

AK47 tracers: red;

I hid the Humvee in an orange grove;

M16 tracers: green;

they will retreat from our land, and collect the bodies of their sons back to America;

I said *shukran* when Mini-Mohammad brought falafel;

we stopped men on the road & took their shovels;

a man covered his daughter's eyes when we entered the room;

during a commercial I carry you to bed;

I carefully tuck the fluff checkered quilt smooth across your naked shoulders & neck;

Saddam would kill all Ali Baba, Karim said, *America soft*;

we were afraid of loose dirt;

I closed my eyes when I passed brick-piles;

two boys sold fake Rolexes at the bridge over the Tigris;

I couldn't open my eyes without sunglasses;

I changed my socks twice a day;

the old man said, *we don't want to be the 51st state*;

generators hummed us to sleep;

as a civilian I hold this remote;

the white plush carpet between my toes;

my hands & neck still red from that sun;

in the TV glare I turn my head & see the snow through the window
;

when the TVs off the room's flushed with dawn's light;

after patrols I topped off the Humvee's fuel tank;

show me America's Babylon, he said, *they were nothing when we ruled the world*;

shots fired disappeared into desert hills;

a civilian said, *you been living under I-Rock?*

the desert stunned my eyes like snow;

we said the sand was *bright, golden, shimmering*;

the boy dreams a missile buries his house in sand;

the boy dreams he rubs & rubs his eyes but the sand won't go away;

The Leg

—north of Balad Ruz

On the road that weaves between the dark desert
a small car moves slow. We watch it closely, rifles
aimed, because one light beams into the hills

from its passenger-window. We wave it down to stop.
One man drives this blue Volkswagen, its doors
held shut with string; another man holds a spotlight

through the open window. We search: no shovels, no rifles,
not even the usual knife for shearing sheep. I walk the men
to our terp, whose face is covered, all but his eyes,

with a black scarf. The men speak & the terp tells us
they've been hired by the phone company—
each night they drive while shining the light, watching

for anyone who might cut the wires, blow the lines.
Kenson says, *What do they do if they see someone?*
The terp speaks & the man who had held the light

runs to the car, leans his body through the open window
& jumps out holding—it must've been sawed-off
from a dining room table—a thick polished wooden leg.

The man smiles & swings the leg left & right.
When he spins across the road as he swings, not showing
any sign that he'll stop, as if wanting to demonstrate

the capability of this table-leg, all of us—the platoon,
the Iraqis—laugh, hard laughs that go deep into the desert.
Even the terp, always scared for his life, mouths out

long screeches, one hand over his mouth. Just south,
a few hours away, the terp had told us—Babylon, & then,
because he'd asked, we'd said our unit hailed from Ohio,

named after the Iroquois, *ohi-yo'*—"good river." In two weeks,
the Coalition Provisional Authority would transfer power
to the Interim Iraqi Government, & the terp thought

the country would explode. Earlier, we'd explained to him
car doors in America covered with yellow ribbon magnets,
but he didn't get it. So, now, as Kenson points to the Volkswagen's

door, says, *Here, they stick, they stick*, the terp shakes
his head while we—though it's getting late—keep laughing,
some of us to tears, as the man keeps swinging the leg.

Service

Bright with light, the flag
ripples on the Jumbotron
as they ask those who've served

to stand. Stand to be
honored. Stand for us to show
our appreciation. Please,

stand. *Come on, stand,*
my friend Sal says. So I stand
with other men who stand

in ball caps & button-up jerseys
in the many sections & rows.
Some fans, holding plastic trays of nachos

& cardboard carriers with jumbo Cokes,
move to their seats quickly,
hunching, embarrassed, not wanting

to take credit for serving
from those who did, from those who stand.
Some stand still & just salute

the digitized wind-whipped flag.
Some with hands in their pockets
twist to see others in the park

who also stand. In the service
I always stood when officers
entered a room. In the service I served

more than thirty days in a combat zone
which qualified me to wear
the combat patch.

After the service, they always asked
where'd you serve. *The Sandbox?*
The Stan? The Storm? In the service

I often serviced my weapon. I served
boiled carrots on Kitchen Patrol
& some mornings I served

by stirring shit to make it
burn better. I served
by closing my eyes

during IED steel & smoke. I served
by running through a marsh
into a home through a doorway

of blue linen hanging
like a piece of laundry—inside
I served by opening each drawer,

each cabinet, looking for wires
& weapons while women screamed in a room
where we'd put them with the children

away from the men
we'd put in another room
to be watched while we searched. I served

by handing out peppermint candies
to children in villages
as fathers & mothers stood in doorways

not speaking, even though if they did
we'd never know what they were saying.
I served standing on dirt streets,

pacing through alleys & avenues
with thumb on the safety
past furious dogs & children

who'd wave or run
even as I, sometimes, just stood
doing nothing but waving

with my left hand
in a constant light, that same
sunlight that makes this little

blond-haired girl glow
as she holds a microphone
with two hands at home plate

while the entire stadium now stands
then everyone, suddenly,
goes silent to hear her sing.

On a Jalawla Street

Too easy, they said, to say the man's bruised face

was like
a plum's cold skin. Cold,

blue plum, I'd written. Plus,

those plums made them think
of Williams' plums. & did

   we want that?   Here's what happened:

we'd heard shouts from somewhere near

the police station. Shouts, I mean, screams. I mean,
a sound that tore through Jalawla's curfew: just a man

yelling for his dear
fucking life.
We saw six, maybe seven,

police in a small circle. On the ground: the man
  in the middle of the circle.

The men kicked, kicked
  whatever limb or hip or ear just happened

to be there
as the man writhed & shook. Very

  carefully,
an officer turned his rifle—holding the muzzle
with both hands—then he swung it

like you'd swing
a tennis racquet? Perhaps,
a baseball bat? But

the man kept moving, ducking. So the officer just stopped

the useless swinging & instead
smashed the wooden butt straight

to the man's bloodied face.
Through flashes

in that space where the officer pulled back
the rifle so he

could load up to do it again,
I saw the face: blood & blue skin shining

in the dark like skin
on a plum (though, I did not think:
plum).

Our Lt. yelled & pushed through the circle

as the officer, now tired, put in one, two, three,
more.   The man breathed heavily.

As he lay there in his own piss, I saw his eyes shut,
sealed with swollen skin   (this isn't to say

this incident—just one small
evening event—is to showcase some soldiers

saving men
from beatings. We,
mostly, weren't).

This is just to say
how that man's face looked
but what's it matter?

Doctor Williams,
maybe, could've fixed

that face (we do know: after eating

those plums—the plums

   that weren't his—he's sorry.
He is.
He even asks for forgiveness).

Intravenous

The smoke's a black rope
rising from the village. How many days

did I sit in the barracks at Bragg
staring at maps of this place

as if it'd save me? On this street,
I couldn't say, in the roar

of police sirens & mosque music,
which way's east, west, which way's

the river. Doc's on his knees
beside the white Opel's

open door. The girl,
months old, screams, the glass

spread around her like rock salt
on the seat cushions. Blue leggings wet,

stuck to the skin with her
own blood. *Light*, Doc says. *Light.*

I lift the M4. Doc scissors the cotton sleeve,
pushes his thumb to her arm

for a vein. Nothing. He brushes back
the dozen or so black hair strands

& finds it: eye to hairline,
pulsing. *See?* he says. *See?*

His fat hand grips her head hard,
flexing the vessel. On that smooth

forehead the vein runs
in a curve that's like, for a moment,

the Tigris I've seen on maps.
   It's not. I know. I keep

my rifle pointed through the shattered
window as cars filled

with wounded weave around us
in the dust. *Hold still*, Doc says.

Then he lowers, slowest thing
I've ever seen, the needle to this blue-

green vein, & I keep the M4s
mounted light aimed—a small

yellow ray beaming
from below the barrel—

steady, toward her head
in Doc's hand, to help him see.

Letter to Lieutenant Owen from the Twenty-First Century

—9/3/13 New Concord, OH

Still children ardent for some desperate
glory, aiming guns at Baghdad before
we're twenty. Midwest in America (you haven't
been): the reds & yellows of leaves swarm
the streets' curbs as the State talks of bombs
they'll send as a message. Simple, sir,
to drop them where you're not. Damascus—
City of Jasmine—shelled with Sarin.
What's changed since your World
War, which still we call *The Great*? Today
we name them Operations. Each speech ends
God bless America. Through the panes
of your mask that man still drowns.
& still, the soldiers: not dead, just *Fallen*.

One morning they gassed us, only once,
in northern Kentucky where America keeps
its bullion behind barbed wire. We danced—
we were made to—in a room where white steam
crawled along the walls & then we slipped
off our masks: it was like the needles of a pine
brushing my iris. Burning skin. We yelled
our Socials with snot-strings on our chins.
As you said, sir, it is sweet & right
to huff gas for one's country, to shave
for one's country because, otherwise,
the mask won't seal. Can you believe,
sir, a death from stubble? & isn't that
something: City of Jasmine. Can you imagine?

Notes

For these poems I consulted the following sources:

".50-Cal. Gunner": The rapper 50 Cent's song, "In Da Club." Anthony Shadid's *Night Draws Near.*

"In Country": Army Regulations 670-1, "Uniforms and Insignia." Michael Herr's *Dispatches.*

"Civilian Notes": Asne Seierstad's *A Hundred and One Days: Fear and Friendship in the Heart of a War Zone.* A May 17, 1998 *ABC News* interview, conducted by John Miller, with Osama bin Laden.

"Letter to Lieutenant Owen from the Twenty-First Century": Wilfred Owen's "Dulce et Decorum Est." The Syrian city of Damascus is often referred to as "The City of Jasmine" (see Nizar Qabbani's "Jasmine Scent of Damascus").

"The Leg" is dedicated to Garrett Harp & Endre Szentkiralyi's 3rd Period Literature at Nordonia High School.

Acknowledgments

Boston Review: "Suspicious Duffel Bag, LSA Anaconda";

The Cincinnati Review (miCRo): "Iraq Good";

Connotation Press: An Online Artifact: "All of This Ammo" (as "Fifty-Caliber Scarf"), "Wave of Bombings";

FIELD: "The Leg," "Frisking Two Men in Sadiyah";

The Gettysburg Review: "In Country";

Harpur Palate: "Letter to Lieutenant Owen from the Twenty-First Century";

The Iowa Review: Winner of the Jeff Sharlet Memorial Award for Veterans (selected by Robert Olen Butler): "Intravenous," "Fort Knox" (as "The Neck in Front of You"), "Test Fire," "Operation New Dawn";

The Journal: "Indirect Fire";

Labor: A Working Class History of the Americas: "Civilian Notes" (as "Civilian Poem");

The New Republic: "Burn Detail";

The New Yorker: ".50-Cal. Gunner" (I. Anthem);

Poetry Daily (reprinted from *Boston Review*): "Suspicious Duffel Bag, LSA Anaconda";

Southeast Review: ".50-Cal. Gunner" (III. Sandbag Detail);

Southern Humanities Review: "Man on a Cart";

Talking River: "On a Jalawla Street," "Mini-Mohammad," "Sunday in the City of Oranges";

TriQuarterly: "Service";

War, Literature & the Arts: "Lana," ".50-Cal. Gunner" ("II. 0000–0400 Hours: Guard Duty with Elbow"; "IV. Iraqi Civil Defense Corps"; "V. Route Willow, Jalawla Bridge"; "VI. ICDC HQ Building"; "VII. Tigris Crossing").

"Sorrow Awareness Training": Honorable Mention, 2012 Robinson Jeffers Tor House Prize for Poetry.

"Intravenous" appeared on *PBS NewsHour* as the Weekly Poem.

Thank you to the many people who encouraged and supported me during the writing of this book. Many heartfelt thanks to everyone at BOA Editions, Ltd. Thank you, specifically, to Peter Conners, Ron Martin-Dent, Kelly Hatton, Sandy Knight, and Jack Langerak. Thank you to the Iraqi artist, Hanaa Malallah, for allowing me to use her incredible work for the cover.

I am extremely grateful for the time I had during a Wallace Stegner Fellowship at Stanford University. Those two years were crucial as I drafted many of the poems in this book. I am even more grateful for so many of the brilliant writers I was able to spend time with while in the program. A very sincere thank you to my teachers: Eavan Boland, Ken Fields, Simone Di Piero, Doug Powell, and Toby Wolff. In my workshop year, thank you especially to Jacques J. Rancourt, Kimberly Grey, Solmaz Sharif, and Austin Smith. Thank you to Greg Wrenn, Kai Carlson-Wee, Michael Shewmaker, Rosi Moffett, Matt Moser Miller, John W. Evans, Mario Chard, Allison Davis, Dana Koster, Mira Rosenthal, Chi Elliott, Tom Kealey, and Christina Ablaza. For his friendship and for his invaluable feedback and for his many readings of this book and for so much more I can't put on the page—thank you, Christopher Kempf. For her honesty and her intelligence and her friendship and for her many readings of this book and so much more, thank you, Corey Van Landingham.

My gratitude to everyone in the English Department at Gettysburg College where I was fortunate enough to grow as a teacher and work with truly brilliant, outstanding colleagues. Thank you, especially, to Kathryn Rhett, Fred Leebron, Nadine Meyer, and Dusty Smith. Thank you to Jody Rosensteel, Joyce Topper, Chris Fee, Will Lane, Suzanne Flynn, Rob Garnett, Doug Miller, Joanne Myers, McKinley Melton, and Stefanie Sobelle.

This collection wouldn't exist without the support of many friends I am very lucky to have: thank you, Whit Arnold, for your friendship and conversations and humor and for giving me your number at Muskingum. Thank you, Kelsey Liebenson-Morse, for all of your insight and patience and spirit and words. Thank you, Meg Thompson and Todd Warhola, for your friendship and conversations and generosity from New Concord to Wellington and beyond. Thank you, Brandon Davis Jennings, for all of your encouragement and no-nonsense attitude and for keeping us out of trouble in Prague. For her generous feedback and her help with this book's title, thank you to Christine Adams. Thank you to the following writers and teachers and friends for more than I can explain: Jane Varley, Norman Dubie, Sally Ball, Cynthia Hogue, Alberto Rios, Preston Hood, Fernando Perez, Ryland Taylor, and Bruce Weigl. More recently, thank you for the support and wisdom from my teachers and colleagues at Ohio University. Many thanks to Dinty W. Moore, Eric LeMay, and Mark Halliday. I am sincerely grateful for a Graduate Summer Scholarship from Ohio University which allowed me to attend the UMASS-Boston William Joiner Center's 2017 conference and workshop. A heartfelt thank you to the entire board and staff at Yaddo for granting me a residency where I was able to work on many of these poems. Thank you to the Sewanee Writers' Conference for a 2013 Fellowship which allowed me to attend workshops and readings with so many outstanding writers.

Thank you to my family for their support of all my writing endeavors. Thank you to my dad, and to my brother, Kenny. Thank you, for too much to name over the years, to Aunt Jane. All of my love to my mother—you are always missed.

About the Author

Hugh Martin grew up in northeast Ohio and joined the Army National Guard in June 2001 as an M1A1 Tanker. He deployed to Iraq in 2004 and after returning home he graduated from Muskingum University. Martin is the author of *The Stick Soldiers* (BOA Editions, Ltd., 2013), winner of the 2011 A. Poulin Jr. Poetry Prize, and the chapbook, *So, How Was the War?* (Kent State UP, 2010). He is the recipient of a Yaddo residency, a Wallace Stegner Fellowship from Stanford University, a Sewanee Writers' Conference Fellowship, a Prague Summer Program Fellowship, and he was the inaugural winner of the *Iowa Review* Jeff Sharlet Award for Veterans. His poetry and essays appear in *The New Yorker*, *The New York Times*, *Grantland*, *The American Poetry Review*, *The Kenyon Review*, and many other publications. He received an MFA from Arizona State University and he was the 2014–15 Emerging Writer Lecturer at Gettysburg College. He is currently a doctoral student at Ohio University.

BOA Editions, Ltd.
American Poets Continuum Series

Colophon

BOA Editions, Ltd., a not-for-profit publisher of poetry and other literary works, fosters readership and appreciation of contemporary literature. By identifying, cultivating, and publishing both new and established poets and selecting authors of unique literary talent, BOA brings high-quality literature to the public. Support for this effort comes from the sale of its publications, grant funding, and private donations.

The publication of this book is made possible, in part, by the support of the following individuals:

Anonymous
Angela Bonazinga & Catherine Lewis
Chris & DeAnna Cebula
Gwen & Gary Conners
Susan DeWitt Davie
Gouvernet Arts Fund
Melissa Hall & Joe Torre
Art & Pam Hatton
Sandi Henschel, *in honor of Sarah Rebecca and Chris Sortino*
Jack & Gail Langerak
Joe McElveney
Boo Poulin
Deborah Ronnen & Sherman Levey
Steven O. Russell & Phyllis Rifkin-Russell
Allan & Melanie Ulrich
William Waddell & Linda Rubel,
in honor of Simah, Ethan, and Jeehye

IN COUNTRY

POEMS

HUGH MARTIN

AMERICAN POETS CONTINUUM SERIES, NO. 169
BOA EDITIONS, LTD. ★ ROCHESTER, NY ★ 2018

First Edition
18 19 20 21 7 6 5 4 3 2 1

For information about permission to reuse any material from this book, please contact The Permissions Company at www.permissionscompany.com or e-mail permdude@gmail.com.

Publications by BOA Editions, Ltd.—a not-for-profit corporation under section 501 (c) (3) of the United States Internal Revenue Code—are made possible with funds from a variety of sources, including public funds from the Literature Program of the National Endowment for the Arts; the New York State Council on the Arts, a state agency; and the County of Monroe, NY. Private funding sources include the Lannan Foundation; the Max and Marian Farash Charitable Foundation; the Mary S. Mulligan Charitable Trust; the Rochester Area Community Foundation; the Ames-Amzalak Memorial Trust in memory of Henry Ames, Semon Amzalak, and Dan Amzalak; and contributions from many individuals nationwide. See Colophon on page 104 for special individual acknowledgments.

ART WORKS.
arts.gov

State of the Arts

NYSCA

Cover Design: Sandy Knight
Cover Art: "US Modern Flag" by Hanaa Malallah
Interior Design and Composition: Richard Foerster
Manufacturing: McNaughton & Gunn
BOA Logo: Mirko

Library of Congress Cataloging-in-Publication Data

Names: Martin, Hugh, 1984- author.
Title: In country : poems / by Hugh Martin.
Description: First edition. | Rochester, NY : BOA Editions, Ltd., 2018. |
  Series: American poets continuum series ; no. 169
Identifiers: LCCN 2018015162 (print) | LCCN 2018018261 (ebook) | ISBN
  9781942683711 (ebook) | ISBN 9781942683704 (pbk. : alk. paper)
Subjects: LCSH: Iraq War, 2003-2011—Poetry.
Classification: LCC PS3613.A7788 (ebook) | LCC PS3613.A7788 A6 2018
(print) |
  DDC 811/.6—dc23
LC record available at https://lccn.loc.gov/2018015162

BOA Editions, Ltd.
250 North Goodman Street, Suite 306
Rochester, NY 14607
www.boaeditions.org
A. Poulin, Jr., Founder (1938–1996)